THE WORLD AROUND YOU

SHAPES AT THE PARK

by
Christianne Jones

PEBBLE
a capstone imprint

Published by Pebble, an imprint of Capstone
1710 Roe Crest Drive, North Mankato, Minnesota 56003
capstonepub.com

Library of Congress Cataloging-in-Publication Data
Names: Jones, Christianne C., author. Title: Shapes at the park / by Christianne Jones
Description: North Mankato, Minnesota : Pebble, an imprint of Capstone, 2022. |
Series: The world around you | Audience: Ages 5-8 | Audience: Grades K-1 |
Summary: "From rectangular ladders to circular rings and hexagonal picnic tables,
the park is full of shapes! Finding shapes adds even more fun to a day at the park,
and early learners will be fully engaged with the interactive, rhyming text and colorful
photos in this picture book"—Provided by publisher. Identifiers: LCCN 2021028441 (print)
| LCCN 2021028442 (ebook) | ISBN 9781663976482 (hardcover) | ISBN 9781666326437
(paperback) | ISBN 9781666326444 (pdf) | ISBN 9781666326468 (kindle edition)
Subjects: LCSH: Parks—Juvenile literature. | Shapes—Juvenile literature. Classification:
LCC SB481.3 .J66 2022 (print) | LCC SB481.3 (ebook) | DDC 333.78/3—dc23 LC record
available at https://lccn.loc.gov/2021028441 LC ebook record available at https://lccn.
loc.gov/2021028442

Editorial Credits
Editor: Christianne Jones; Designer: Brann Garvey; Media Researcher: Svetlana Zhurkin;
Production Specialist: Laura Manthe

Image Credits
Dreamstime: Annachizhova, 3, Pavelbalanenko, 19, Thomas Bullock, 16; Shutterstock:
2xSamara.com, top Cover, Afonkin_Y, bottom left 29, Africa Studio, 24, Andrew Angelov,
middle left 29, Backgroundy, top left 29, Dmitry Bruskov, bottom Cover, Fernando
Avendano, top right 29, GABLIYA ALISA, 18, gob_cu, middle right 29, gorosan, spread
14-15, gpointstudio, bottom right 13, greenland, bottom 6, Kartashova, top left 28,
LightField Studios, top left 13, MaLija, 27, Mehmed Birkov, bottom right 28, Noam
Armonn, 22, Oksana Volina, top 6, Patrick Foto, 7, Purple Clouds, 21, Sergey Novikov, 11,
Sinan.AYHAN, bottom left 28, Sunflower Aoi, bottom right 29, Tom Hartrey, top right 28,
Victoria Tucholka, 12, Viktor Birkus, 23, William Booth, 20,
Yuliya Evstratenko, 25, Yuricazac, spread 8-9

Special thanks to Sveta Zhurkin and Dan Nunn for their consulting work and help.

SO MANY SHAPES

Pointy or round. Big or small.

Lots of sides or no sides at all.

Head to the park for a colorful display

of shapes just waiting for you to play!

2-D SHAPES

Two-dimensional (2-D) shapes are flat.
They have a front and a back.

circle

square

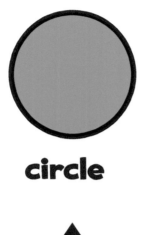

triangle

rectangle

trapezoid

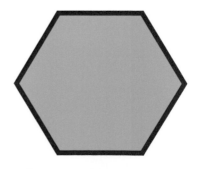

hexagon

3-D SHAPES

Three-dimensional (3-D) shapes are solid. They can have a front, a back, and sides that are called faces.

cube

rectangular prism

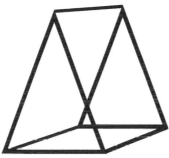

triangular prism

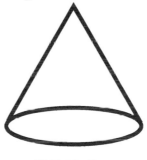

cone

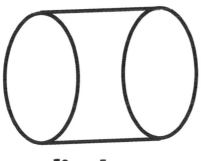

cylinder

sphere

circles

Circles have no corners and are perfectly round.

There are lots of places in the park for **circles** to be found.

squares

Squares have four sides that are all the same.
Draw lots of **squares** to make a jumping game.

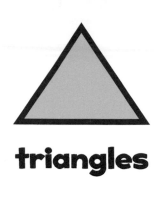

triangles

Triangles have three corners and three sides. Fly a kite in the wind to see a **triangle** glide!

rectangles

Rectangles have two sides that are short and two that are long.

Take a break, play on a swing, or climb to show you're strong.

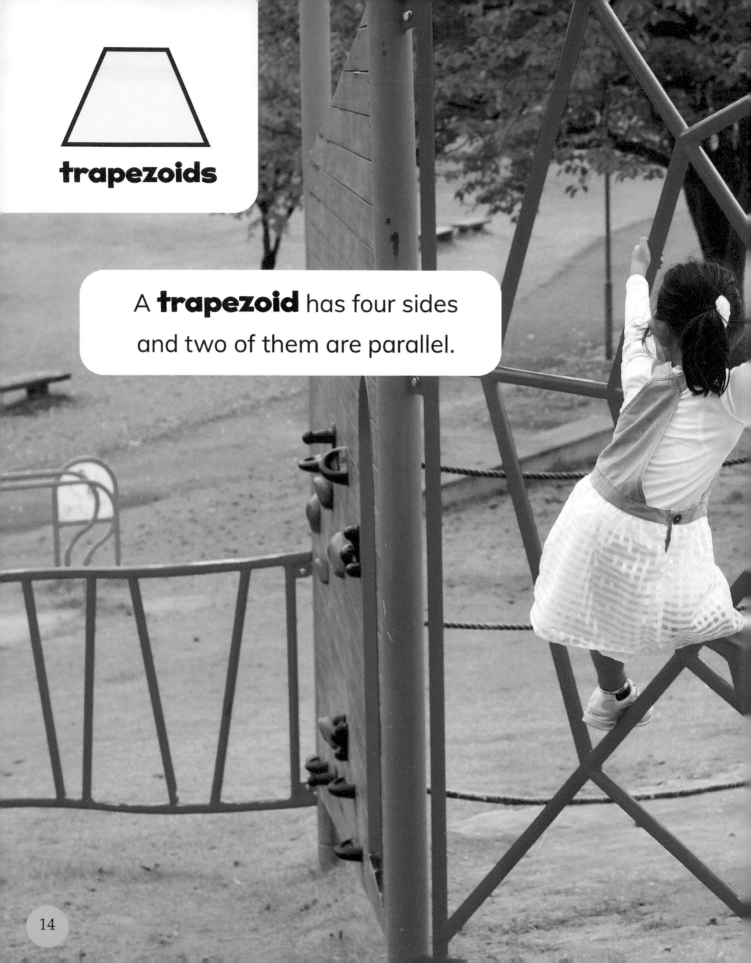

trapezoids

A **trapezoid** has four sides and two of them are parallel.

This park has a climbing web made from **trapezoids**. Can you tell?

hexagons

A **hexagon** has six angles and six sides.
It can be the starting point for a crazy slide!

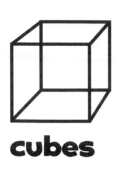

cubes

A **cube** has six identical faces. It looks like a box.

Play a game of tic-tac-toe or spin the colorful blocks.

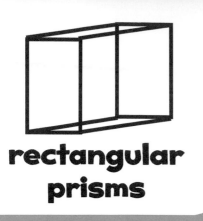

rectangular prisms

A **rectangular prism** has six faces—
four rectangular and two square.
Can you move from block to block
by jumping through the air?

triangular prisms

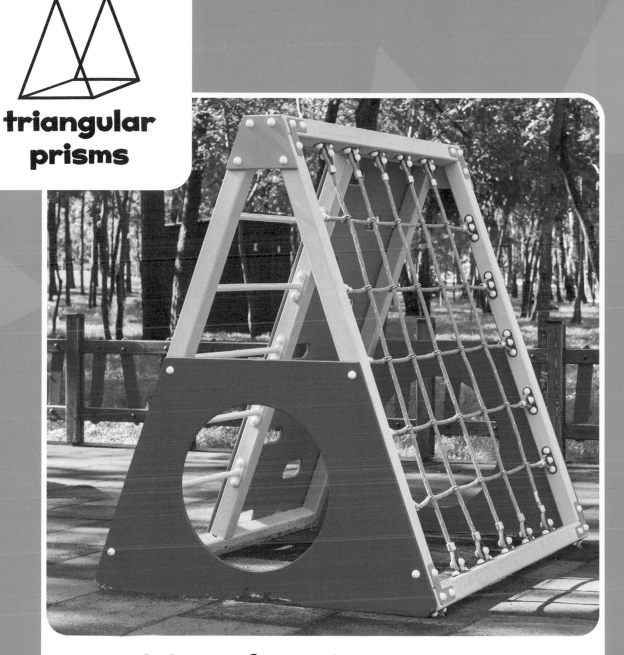

A **triangular prism** has two triangle
bases and three rectangular sides.
You can climb or crawl through this
fun frame—you get to decide!

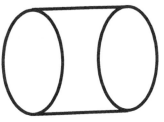

cylinders

A **cylinder** is round with a circle
at the bottom and the top.
When on its side it can spin
until you make it stop.

cones

A **cone** has a point and a circular base.

A spin on one will bring a smile to your face.

spheres

A **sphere** is round and not flat at all.

Spheres are floating bubbles and bouncing balls.

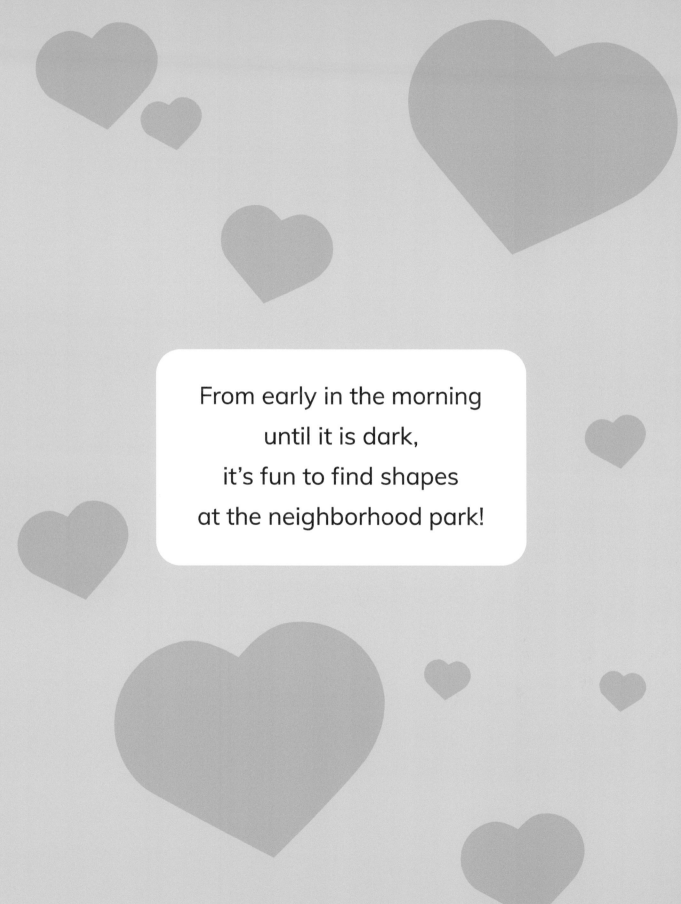

From early in the morning
until it is dark,
it's fun to find shapes
at the neighborhood park!

NAME THE SHAPES QUIZ

The answers can be found on page 30.

2-D OR 3-D QUIZ

sphere

squares

cone

rectangles

hexagons

cylinders

The answers can be found on page 31.

NAME THE SHAPES QUIZ ANSWERS

1. The colorful rings are **circles**.

2. The picnic tables are **hexagon** shaped. They each have six sides.

3. The climbing frame has lots of **trapezoid** shapes on the net.

4. The playhouse has lots of shapes! Did you spot a **triangle**, a **rectangle**, and a **square**?

2-D OR 3-D QUIZ ANSWERS

The net **squares**, the climbing frame **rectangles**, and the **hexagon** paving stones are **2-D shapes**. They are flat.

The ball, or **sphere**, the ice cream **cone**, and the **cylinder** slides are **3-D shapes**. They are solid.

LOOK FOR THE OTHER BOOKS IN THE WORLD AROUND YOU SERIES!

 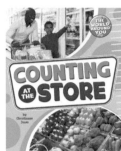  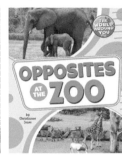 

AUTHOR BIO

Christianne Jones has read about a bazillion books, written more than 70, and edited about 1,000. Christianne works as a book editor and lives in Mankato, Minnesota, with her husband and three daughters.